Sixteen Summers

Celia Maddison

1940 -

Pentland Books
Edinburgh • Cambridge • Durham • USA

First published in 2001 by
Pentland Books
1 Hutton Close
South Church
Bishop Auckland
Durham

British Library Cataloguing in Publication Data.
A Catalogue record for this book is available
from the British Library.

ISBN 1 85821 881 0

Typeset by CBS, Martlesham Heath, Ipswich, Suffolk
Printed and bound by Antony Rowe Ltd., Chippenham

DEDICATION

'Parted friends again may meet,
from the toils of nature free.
Crowned with mercy. Oh, how sweet,
will eternal friendship be.'

C. W. Thomson

To the memory of my dear late Mother, and Audrey Chapman,
who both passed away during the time of writing.

FOREWORD

I am not a yellow belly, although I am married to one. My family and I moved to this village, close to the Wash, some forty five years ago and I have lived here off and on ever since. Dad bought a shop and post office, he was also the Sunday newspaper distributor for the district. With such a background I quickly came to meet and know everyone in and around the village at a time when practically every inhabitant, men, women and children, worked on the farms. There were still grass fields and hedgerows then, electricity and running water were still a novelty. People seldom left the village even for a holiday, a day out in Skeg. or Boston was a treat to be anticipated for weeks. Everyone spoke with the broadest of Lincolnshire accents, which was practically foreign to an incomer like me. The world seemed full of larger than life characters who could spin yarns about people and events to keep a listener enthralled for hours. There was Billy Jackson, Grannie Epton, Boko Simpson and now there is Celia.

John Ghest

INTRODUCTION

'I'm not too happy about it, Mrs Simpson, you really ought to have a midwife present,' the local doctor had told my Mother when I came into the world.

I was told much later that she had been detained at another birth, just down the road from us - must have been a good year.

Still, Mother had sent for Granny Baker, who had plenty of experience in such matters. Just in case the midwife had not turned up at all.

It turned out okay in the end. I was all right. No not all right but, some of us aren't, a lot of us have a screw loose.

Still I have had a decent life - bleached by the sun - and it has been, up to this moment in time, certainly worth all that hassle that took place in the back bedroom all those years ago, during the second year of the war - the last war, not the first.

Perhaps, though, some of you probably wish that I was dead already, and 'down there'.

Right now though, I should think that heaven is a lonely place. Either way, I shall probably come back to haunt you.

I

School, Home, and Friends

I would be about four years old, when I was sent to the infant school, and round the 'wyking's' would go the flannel to get rid of the breakfast crumbs. then I would be route-marched across our footbridge at the front of our house. I expect that it had seen a few thousand footprints through the years – some good, some bad. Funny how we always remember the not so good ones – one of them I do recall . . .

'Don't swing on our door,' Father said to the little girl – her mother was collecting some club money, and Father, who was normally cool and collected, paid the rest of what we were owing and told 'em, in a manner not befitting himself, to not come here anymore. Now that I am sure of, they are now 'clubbing' it up with the angels.

I would stay at the infant school until I was about eight, and then it was up to the local 'prison' and the dastardly 'warder's' at the 'C of E' at Friskney Church End, where I was a 'don't like it'.

I was never able to fulfil a dream, to drown the whole lot of 'em – the teaching fraternity that is – somewhere in the Adriatic I believe. But it never came to be. Pity really, it would have been worth it to see them gasp for breath. Mind you with my luck, some of them would be able to swim anyway.

A large fire in the infant schoolroom kept all us kids warm in the wintertime and the protective pines – they are still there – were hovering over us small specks of human-kind – a point of gathering for brighter stars.

And I am still wondering where the tower-bell went to, when the sky darkens, as it did then, during the turbulent times of the war and early childhood, in the forties.

The butter would be wiped off with the crumbs – we were lucky, we did have butter and, come to think of it, we hardly went short at all – that had managed to get round from ear to ear, then it would be a quick wash at night during the week, with a better wash at the week-end.

During the time we were small, we were not allowed to get a wash by ourselves, as we might spill water on the floor – we had one of the cleanest places in the parish. It was not easy trying to get one's arse in an enamel bowl, but we managed it somehow. There would be a ring round us for days.

I suppose that when the place was built, it would have had a fair amount of 'modern' things of the day, whereas the people with a better income had been in that position for several years.

Next door to the kitchen was a wash-house where the only entrance was from the outside, and it wasn't very pleasant when the weather was a bit on the inclement side and the door would blow shut, if you forgot to prop it open. It all depended on how much steam you got on, and the small window wasn't able to take it all; in that case of course, the snow would keep blowing in, along with the rest of the bad weather, and Mother would have to stand there washing as best as she could.

Her early life had seen her use a dolly tub, but she had, when

I was young, moved up to a kind of 'semi-automatic' washing machine, where you had to turn a handle in the lid. There was a rubber wringer that also had to be turned and, in time, the coal copper – that was built in at the end of the wash-house – would be replaced by an electric one, which was a lot easier than having to keep shovelling the coal on.

I remember putting my vest in the new electric copper and it coming out as stiff as a board, and then there were bloody 'fireworks' I can tell you.

After dear Mother had no use for either the electric copper or the 'manual' washing machine – which would be in nineteen fifty six – I carried on in the same old fashion till nineteen fifty eight, and then got my first all-electric washing machine that Father bought me. Several moths were killed in the rush.

During the war years, I would be stuck under the table at night and, I can still see Father standing on the door-step, lighting up a fag, while watching various aircraft overhead, on their way out. Lesser numbers would return, sadly.

He cut a solitary figure, with the smoke hovering around us like an autumn mist. A man of few words, but I can imagine that he would certainly be thinking a great deal.

The blind went up at night, tacked to the window frame – the holes were there for years, a grim reminder of how close we came to a direct hit.

Father's idea of 'keeping the home fires burning' was to him just that, he didn't go on many fire-watching stints. I clearly remember him telling me that our place meant more to him than a few snotty farmer's straw-stacks. 'Let em put their own fires out,' he would say – and I can see where he was coming from. I wouldn't exactly call it a romance between the rich and the poor them days, and not even today.

Still old Egbert bear kept me company all through the war, and he still sits on the dressing table, and if I can, without my husband seeing – not that he cares anyway – I will get him in the bed. 'Are you alright Egbert, don't get your head stuck between two pillows, you might hurt yourself,' I say to him. Then ask my husband what would happen if the firemen had to come, and see us all in the bed. He said not to worry, as we were all on the ground floor and would be able to get out.

The old 'whip and top' would be one of my toys then, along with my doll, that the doctor had seen fit to sit on during one of his visits – a leg fell off, but I don't recall him buying me a new one. I would be called in from playing out on the back yard during the day-time raids, clearly remembering being told to get inside.

One or two people that Father knew would come round to our place with the idea of building a sort of shelter in the back dyke, to protect us all from the bombing, but that never got off the ground. Father would listen to the idea, and then they would go away empty-handed, and Dad would light up another fag. He smiled about that for years after – still it might have worked, on reflection.

In my youth, like nearly everybody else in those days – and indeed some still do – before we got a fancy bathroom to wash in – we would all get a wash in front of the fire, an old 'Lumley' grate. Long before that, God knows what they did. It would be a bit parky standing outside round a fire near the cave entrance, although I doubt very much if they got a wash at all. Just up my street, I can't stand the sight of water.

The only trouble with the 'Lumley' was, you had to keep letting the water out with a tap at the side of the fireplace, as the boiler at the back of the grate would get too hot, so most of the time would be spent letting the water out and putting it back again, which seemed a waste of time to me.

One other alternative was to let the fire go down, and then you would 'starve' to death, and Father would have to sit there by the fire – what was left of it – in his army greatcoat, looking as white as a sheet – ashen would be a better word. But we managed until we could get a better grate put in – which is still there, as it happens.

There was electricity when the place was built, but Mother would still cook on the Lumley, till finally getting an electric cooker in the forties.

The day the old grate got on fire, the smoke was going across the road like a steam train, and it covered the pub, the Bricklayer's Arms, several yards away – she wasn't half going at it.

The glow from the metal – with the immense heat – of the grate was shining on the lino under the table, and Father went up to the false roof, to see if the bricks were warm in the chimney-stack – hot would have been a more appropriate term, but there was hardly any heat at all. I clearly remember Mother saying that we ought to throw some water on it – somehow I don't think I would be here now if we had done – still, anything in a fit of panic.

We had no hot and cold water, just a cold tap inside the kitchen and, before that, a pump – a manual one – also in the kitchen, that would take water from a cistern outside the house – don't think that I would relish doing that now, though.

I remember seeing Father cleaning it out and, hell it was deep, and I thought that he was going to drown. Mind you I don't think that it was likely, seeing as there wasn't any water in it at the time. But being young, I was scared stiff. I could just see the top of his head, and really thought that he was going to drown.

Father could have had a bathroom put in when the place was built in the thirties but decided against it – it was going to cost another eighty pounds and he had never been cruel to animals, especially of the order of 'Lepidoptera'. But I had one installed in 1975, when I was thirty-five. And it's a waste of time standing there wondering which bits to wash next. Do I start at the bottom or the top?

It is warm and sunny – it always seemed to be when I was young – as I make my way over to Sandra Wright's house, along the cinder path. Her place was just behind ours and down the dyke I would go – it separated the two places – and up the other side, getting my clean knickers dirty, sliding about in the dyke – which would be mostly pretend, and nothing unusual for me anyway.

I make my way across their garden to their back door, where hopefully Sandra – armed to the teeth with tin lids and water – will come out to play.

Back to sit under the lilac bush we go, and stir all that lovely water in the dust to make enough mud for several pies, and Mother would be none too pleased when I arrived home covered in the stuff – which I often did. But it was lovely, and we enjoyed every minute of it, smoothing the tops of the pies with a knife that Sandra had sneaked from the kitchen when her parents weren't looking – I wasn't allowed a knife, Mother said that I was too small to have one.

After a while we would tire of pie making, and would go on to something else, a large tin of 'Oster milk'. We would be halfway down the tin, when I would be not feeling too well – 'I feel sick' – and I am starting to flag and, I think that Sandra will be the winner. But it tastes delicious – well it did in those days.

An idyllic childhood romance between the two of us for a few short years, before we would grow away from each other, and go our separate ways.

But for those days, there was no question of us thinking about the future, or what it had in mind – we didn't need one, and for then, that would do.

The infant school-house has long since returned to the soil from whence it came. And I remember being given a card, and a poetry book, the card having various pictures of birds on it. Mind you, Mother would not have it in the house, so it had to go to Uncle Sol's place, where it perished through the years, from the damp coming up from under the old brick floor, underneath the chaise longue.

Uncle Sol always had coal missing, and we knew who got it, but we turned a blind eye to it. Even in them days there was a lot of pinching going on, even between so-called friends and neighbours, and not a lot of reporting. There was one family that would go short one Christmas – so I was told years later – if their friends ever got caught, and if my memory serves me right, they were. Mind you, it's a damn sight worse these days.

Uncle Sol, staring out from under his cap, that he hardly ever took off . . .

Sitting in the corner of the room – there was only the one main room downstairs, apart from a small sloping place built on the back. And there he would sit, usually smoking his pipe of 'twist' tobacco, strong as a fummard, or should I say polecat.

After a while, he would, with a mouthful of spit that he had managed to conjure up like magic, get up and go to the grate, and aim straight for the fire – trouble was he would often miss it and the spit would go into the pot hanging from the 'wreaking' hook instead.

The large black pot would, more often than not, have a piece of pork boiling in it – mind you it would give it a bit of flavour, as it always went down a treat between two pieces of dry bread. Funny how we never seemed to bother what we would eat when we were small, even though we had been brought up clean.

He always stood the paraffin stove in the middle of the floor, so he could get 'round' it, he would say – it would have sent me dizzy but, he seemed to like it that way.

An old tin on the top with either rashers or sausages in – the latter of the two had probably been hanging up in the back place till they were green – and hardly any food poisoning at all. I well remember him showing me how to skin a rabbit, not that I thought much about it though. The pheasants would be hung up, with the guts left intact – provided that you could get one without being seen – for a fairly long while, well certainly till they were ripe.

Sol's 'black-lead' grate would gobble up a fair amount of coal at the one go, and he would often chuck paraffin on it to get it going, and the flames would be going out of the chimney, four or five feet in the air. Often he would use a bit of paper – held in front of the fire – to create a draught, holding it, more often than not, too near the fire, and it would go flying out of the top, and I would go running outside to see where it had gone to. It was highly amusing to see it going over next door and out of sight.

Spending a fair amount of time in the pub was never a downfall, but he would come rolling home, drunk as you please.

The beer was a lot cheaper in those days, before the last war, and in Uncle Sol's case, it would have been before the first world war, too.

Cheaper or not, they were no better off in comparison, there is not much difference from today. The wages were low then and in some places they still are.

The day that he decided that he had had enough, was when he thought that the lightning had taken the 'paper' out of his wellingtons – I think that he had gone onto something stronger than beer.

'I think that I am going to learn to ride a bike,' he said – mind you we knew that he had never been on one for years, and we tried to talk him out of it, but all to no avail, he was determined. He managed to get his hands on a clapped-out old thing, all the colours of the rainbow it was. And this particular day he decided to try it out – with almost disastrous results.

It was a woman's bike, which was probably better to get on, or probably not. We all waited with bated breath, as he attempted to get on the thing. He managed that fairly well, and went a few yards down the path, from his front door towards the gate, and he nearly managed to get there when, a few yards from the end

11

of the old track, he went over to the right, and landed sideways in the hedge that parted his place and next door – still astride the bike. I remember him lying there for a few minutes, and said to my Mother 'he's killed himself'. But he scraped himself out of the hedge, and vowed never to get on a bloody bike again. It had put paid to his folly, thank goodness.

There was an enamel bowl, and an earthenware one, on top of a table in the sloping back place, with a bar of carbolic soap at the side.

Food would be kept in there on the shelf – and it had a better 'shelf life' than today. The pigs were fed better them days.

Not having much in the way of utensils, zinc buckets would be the norm, stood at the side of the fireplace, ready to chuck the coal on and it was always warm in there. One reason I suppose would be because the ceilings were low, just a few inches above my head.

Sol's long moustache had a beautiful auburn tint to it, usually because he always drank his tea with no milk in it, and he said that he didn't need any either.

Nor did he need any electricity, and had it taken out when it became more expensive. Then he went back to the old oil lamps instead. Mind you it only went up about two shillings and sixpence. A tender job indeed trying to clean the lamp glass, with a piece of paper and a stick.

The times that I would keep telling him that the wick was too high, as the smoke would be hitting the ceiling. Black as yer hat, it was. 'It's all right, I can't see a bloody thing if it's any lower,' he said.

Never had a tap inside the house, it was just outside the back door.

To some it would be a fairly bleak existence, especially when you had to go to the 'petty' – or toilet, to give it its proper name – outside, at night, at the back of the house. AND when the bucket was full – which it often was – try to find somewhere to bury the contents in a piece of garden not used before, which wasn't easy. He never did manage to get to having a modern water toilet.

I remember Father going down our garden path, carrying the toilet bucket, with the wind blowing the paper off the top, and putting the contents in a hole that had already been dug for the purpose – like I say, if you could find one. I would have to clean the place out, with cobwebs and spiders all over.

Uncle Sol, one of fifteen children, and an elder brother of my late father, would live until his eighty-third year.

He had spent his life working the soil, and I should think that we are all the wiser for his existence.

Take a deserving sleep, you are missed, and nothing of your character can fade.

Well, every year it comes round, and this was no exception: Nancy Chapman and me decided that we would go out and get some pocket money. We would be in our element, a couple of young kids on Guy Fawkes Night, walking down the Eaudykes road in the village of Friskney, where we both lived.

I should think that it would be dusk when we started out and Nancy's Mother, Audrey, would be our 'chaperon', to see that we didn't get up to any mischief. Not that we were likely to, but there was just the possibility that we could have done.

We had been to a few houses that were hardly chucking their

13

money about – the odd penny, or perhaps a sixpence if we were lucky.

I would think that we had been to several places, when we decided to go to poor old Granny B, and left the road to walk down her path – we would only go to the people that we knew, which in those days would probably be nearly all of them – to see if we would have any better luck. She and her husband were getting on a bit, and a decent couple. And I don't see how they could have had a lot. But when you are young, it is a thing that would not come to mind.

Getting dark by then, we left the road and, large as life, we went up their path, leaving Nancy's mother. Seeing as how we could do it by ourselves.

Up to the door at the end of the house – it's still standing but under a different tenant now – and standing side by side, like a couple of soldiers, we started to sing – the only trouble was, we only knew 'Tulips and Heather'. Nothing to do with Guy Fawkes at all. And after we had given our rendition it all went still, and you could hear a pin drop, and we would probably be thinking that no one was coming to the door.

But after what seemed like an eternity, the door opened, and this elderly woman stood there and probably scared us half to death – us being young of course. Mind you, probably grown-ups all had the same effect, looking down on us from a lofty height. 'Here ya are, bairns,' she said – and held out her hand. I did likewise, and she placed a coin of some sort into my palm which I closed forthwith – couldn't let it escape, now could I. 'Now be off we ya,' she said. And I can't remember thanking her, my greed had taken complete control.

She turned round and went inside, while at the same time we

started back down the path, to where Nancy's mother was waiting.

We had only gone a few steps, when I looked into my hand – which had been coming slowly open from when she have given me the coin – and saw a fairly large shining object, that I took to be a shilling. In fact I knew that it was, and I could not contain my excitement all the way back.

I kept saying over and over again 'I've got a shilling' – how greedy can one get. And when we arrived back to the edge of the road, Nancy said to her mother, 'Celia thinks that she has got a shilling.' And I knew that I had, well I mean, what else could it be.

It had been fairly dark at the end of the old house, with the trees and bushes blocking the light – or what was left of it. But out of the shadows, the night sky was a bit brighter and, when we finally got to the road edge, I opened my hand fully and, the three of us gazed down into my palm, huddled round each other, expecting a large windfall. It was then that I realized that – and at the same time I would be struck speechless as well – it wasn't a shilling at all, and my being struck dumb didn't last all that long when I saw what the old bat had given yours truly, as the stillness gave way to . . . 'Oh, the ode bugger, it's only an ha'penny!'

We didn't get a lot of money that night. At one house there was a 'joey' each, for us, which was the highlight of the night – mind you we had to go into their house and sing, and they got 'Tulips and Heather' as well.

Audrey saw me safely home, and when I arrived in our living room, I said to my parents, 'I'm not going there anymore.' To which my Father replied, 'Why, what's the matter, mate?' and then I came out with it. 'Well we've only just come from Granny B and she's only given us a ha'penny, the ode bugger.' To which my Mother said, 'Haw cee, the poor old things probably haven't got much money.' Father said, 'There's some money on the mantelpiece, you can have some of that.'

II

Excursions Near and Far

Skegness was as far as we got in my younger days, it seemed so far that we thought we had gone to the moon. A trek down to the 'Barley Mow' corner near the A52, and a trek across the footpaths to 'boon pit' field, to watch the summer traffic go by and collect car numbers – that would be enough for then, it would suffice.

We would always ask Father where they were going, and he would reply, 'I don't know lass.' Did we believe him? I seem to think that we did, but, perhaps felt disappointed in a way that he didn't tell us, for something seemed to tell me that he knew.

Still I suppose it was a lot easier for Father to say that he didn't have any idea, or else it would have been never-ending.

Leaning over the five-barred gate, in boon pit field, a short distance from the A52, with buses going to 'nowhere' seemed strange to me.

We would watch them for several hours, then take it slowly home for our tea.

Several of the locals in my young days would gather at the 'Mow' corner, of a summer's afternoon, mostly on a Sunday, leaving their bicycles near the pub fence. A strange occupation, but satisfying. Then they would part company, and make their way home again till the next time – perhaps the next week-end.

The men would nearly always put on a better jacket and the women a decent frock and, probably, a better hat, just to make themselves look a bit more presentable, just in case there might be someone there.

In many a home they would be saying 'you can't go out looking like that'. And all just to watch a few cars go by.

Not all, but several of us, would probably live and die within a few miles of that area, and never want for anything else.

The smoke from Father's cigarette might still be blowing across the grassland.

There is now a new occupant living next door to Uncle Sol, in the old 'mud and stud' just across the field from us. That end of the building had been empty for years, after my parents had left it to come in 1937 to where I still live. Dear old Martha Holly would be the new tenant, having been bombed out of Hull.

She had this funny thing strapped to her waist, and something in her ear, that I, a young child, could not understand. To me, then, all it ever did was make a lot of squeaks and groans. Mother explained to me that it was a hearing aid, and that dear old Holly was almost as deaf as a post. I had to shout to make myself heard. 'Don't shout, I'm not deaf,' she said. But I kept telling Mother that she could not hear anything that I said. She hardly ever put a new battery in the thing, only the trouble was that when she did she could hear everything that I said, which I can assure you didn't go down all that well.

Round the parish she would trundle the old 'tansad'. Later

on we would get a Silver Cross pram for my Brother Bruce, who had come along in forty six. Holly would never push this 'other' one, said it was too posh.

Down to the Barley Mow public house at the end of the road where we lived, and then it would be across to the 'stores' the other side of the A52, about a couple of doors away from the pub, where I would be let loose among the family 'heirlooms' – once they would have belonged to someone else – that were in the place, it being a sort of antique shop.

After the war, when she probably thought that I was a bit older, she would have me waving to a Raleigh advert man, on top of an old shed at the end of our road, just opposite the Barley Mow. 'Wave to your boyfriend', she said. Still, it was better than the fat boy from up the road, he would often come past on his bicycle – sadly no longer with us.

That way we would elude time, astride the white fence, opposite my 'boy friend' and then after a long afternoon make our way home, with the 'tansad' full of everything but the sink. My parents knew that we were coming, the wheel of the pram wobbled and squeaked.

It was broken hearts all round when Holly moved to a better house, although we did go and see her most days, especially during the school term, to have our lunch with her.

In your Yorkshire accent, 'if I could fetch you back' . . .

It was some way to the allotment, alongside a drain. It was either the allotment, the footpaths, or the trains and sometimes the marshes, with Brother Bruce wobbling on his bicycle, and Father hanging on to him for dear life. And I was at the rear telling them what to do. 'Mind the drains, for God's sake,' or something along those lines.

Father, who made hope spring eternal, would set the wheels of our existence in motion, on sunny afternoons. We would spend the afternoon in idle curiosity where the clayleaf and the hoe were to meet in battle, and the hollows filled with water, where hardly anything would grow. And I must say that it was anybody's guess. And they, the veg merchant's would often come out with 'things are not making much now'.

Rapturous moments, encased in the dust of Cranberry Lane, born of an obsession to escape to somewhere – and for Father to take us.

It would not last, it never did. No sooner had we arrived than I wanted to go home again, and would sit on a log at the end of the field, singing my rendition of 'Shelly Hay' or Sheila, whoever she was.

Bruce would be messing about with a stick, and Father would be having a struggle with the hoe, and stop and look round, and light another fag – he had to have something to steady his nerves and fags seemed the only thing at the time.

'Can we go into the field next door?' I piped up. It was the same every time, and poor old Father never got much done at all – happy days.

So off we went, looking for poppies in the cornfield next door, with Father tying the petals down, to make a dress.

Trailing him from one place to another, he would say, 'I never git nowt done we you two, I shall leave you both at home next time.' But he never did.

Father had taken his place among a crop that had yielded few fruits. The yellow earth stirred beneath a steel blade. As he manoeuvred between the rows on the sparsely covered ground, his cigarette glowed with every intake of breath.

With almost an art-like quality, he had carefully taken away the twine that had held the hoe in place on the bicycle.

Speaking very few words, he drew his composure from generations before: a man who had worked hard all his life.

The cycle race would be all but won – I mastered the art of staying on some years previous to my twelve years, and I would negotiate the way to the allotment at some speed. One can only speculate that I was given the chance to win and, often ended up amid the splendour of stinging nettles, somewhere at the end of the field. Gallant though I was, in somewhat dulcet tones, I would make it known that I had.

Picking up a stone, I would ask Father what it was, and he would say 'I don't know, bairn, what it is.' And I would turn and saunter off somewhere else, for all of five minutes, with Bruce trailing on behind. After a while I would go back and ask him if he would make us a reed boat, from the reeds at the side of the field, which just happened to be in the bottom of the dyke, and down Father would have to go to get them out, throwing his hoe down in the field.

Father was a master craftsman – mind you, some of them sank without a trace. You had to get the mast right, or over they went. Poking them with sticks when they got stuck behind some reeds didn't hold our attention for long, and we would soon go in with the dive bombers – lumps of muck to the untrained.

That didn't last long, and then it would be 'can we go into the woods, Dad, can we?' Up round the top of the field, into the small copse – until its death came suddenly with the bulldozer – with Father cutting us a stick to swipe with, and me turning into a romantic, gathering the purple violets when I wasn't looking at the sky, which would stare down through the trees, that were standing tall as sentinels, while our feet would press the still woodland floor.

Cranberry Lane would see us over several years of our adventures. And after would be silent of our voices. Silent of steel against the amber soil. No more ships that would sail close to the edge of the world, or violets in clammy hands. Nor cricket matches, or my feet shuffling in the dust.

It is left to be consumed by those who will find their own niche there, this will be their time.

There is a vast expanse of fenland still out there, and I often quietly think of it.

Father's bone-handled pocket knife lies in a drawer. The day it had cut a lump of sugar-beet, Brother Bruce and I would have been across the footpath near our home. Most Sundays when the weather was fine, you would see us going across between the fields. 'Git it down yer, lass,' Father would say, as he cut a piece of beet with the worn-out blade. 'A bit of muck won't hurt yer,' he said. And I should imagine that it would get washed in a puddle, or probably wiped on the grass – we weren't picky at all, even though we had been brought up clean. Mind you, them days it would not have been sprayed with pesticide – well hardly ever.

Had anyone ever bothered to inspect the crops, they would have found that some of it was missing, usually it was of course whatever was in season at the time. We would mill our own ears of corn, and let the wind take care of the rest. And Mr X would have holes in his carrots, just as if some animal had taken a bite out of them – strange that there would be no teeth marks.

Dad would finish up carrying the guinea pig – and it wasn't house trained. Heaven knows why I took it, but it had to go along with us. Most of our pets had funny names, and this one was no exception.

There were three guinea pigs through the years, Guts, Bowels and Thomas and mine was the 'Guts' one.

The dust would swirl around our feet on the dry summer days, usually stirred up by us playing steam trains, and chuffing along, and we would go home covered in the dust.

Not very often would we meet anyone, as people hardly ever worked on a Sunday, not like now, they hardly know one day from another, which is sad really.

The three of us would trek across, slowly but surely wending our way right to the corner of boon-pit field, and down the side of the field to see if the cows were there. Yes it would be the same old thing, but we would never tire of it, and I wish that I was still doing it now.

I was the more adventurous of the three of us, usually walking through the crops of some farmer or other. I would be mowing down the corn – mind you, they wouldn't see me all that well, especially if the corn was a bit on the tall side, me being a bit on the small side.

Grass snakes sleeping in the sun, and a willow tree, with the 'blood' of Christ, supposedly, on it – it was of course the seed.

Father would keep lighting his fags, and the smoke would blend in with the smell of his cloth jacket, which he nearly always wore – that and his cloth cap, which went well with his old trousers, a lovely homely smell, that I shall not find easy to forget.

There was a kind of romance between us that can no longer exist, but on the seventh day, one might see his ghost walking across the footpath, and if you look closely, sometime in the future, you might see two smaller shapes, somewhere about.

Out come the bicycles, and Father, Bruce and I, would head off in the direction of Friskney sea lane. Right down to the bottom, and over the second sea 'bank' which was meant to keep the sea away from coming over on to the land and, I suppose, has nearly always succeeded, apart from the odd high tide that has come pretty close to taking its own way in the scheme of things.

It was lovely over the bank with acres of marsh grasses, and heather – not there now though, sadly.

Paddling in the endless creeks in the warm water, and then sitting on the side, dangling our feet, and watching the crabs on the bottom. Some of the pools were fairly deep, and would change with the tidal current from one day to the next, but Father would be there to keep an eye on us.

My skirt above my knees, and Bruce with his short trousers rolled even shorter, we would go out in that fashion, following the tide almost to 'low water', which to some might seem a dangerous liaison, and I suppose that it could have been if you didn't use a certain amount of common sense.

Gather the handful of heather to bring home, along with anything else that you could find. Usually something that had been washed up by the tide, even if it had been dead for ages. Then Father would 'create' and tell us to put it down and leave it where it was – not that we took any notice of him though, and we would usually finish up with a pile of rubbish at home, which would get burned at a later date, more's the pity.

Poor old Dad would say 'I'm not carting that lot home,' but he ended up doing it all the same. Sometimes it would only be a piece of stick which we wanted to keep – either way none of it was of much importance, well not to grown-ups anyway.

There would be more than that to deal with, like the time I came a cropper, falling off my bicycle, just after we had ridden over the top of the bank, and were going down the other side on our way home, and I would be practising 'leaving go' of the bike handle-bars and, fell off to the left, as I recall, and almost finished up in a dyke, or 'delf' as we called it. And failing that, it would have been the concrete end of the tunnel sticking out. But I managed to do neither, although you should have seen the state of my knees, they were bandaged for weeks after that.

At some later date 'our' sea bank would be taken down, and I should say that even though it was not removed, it might as well have been, seeing as we were not able to go to our favourite stamping ground anymore. While two more 'banks' would be put up farther out, supposedly to protect us all even more from the sea, and one cannot help but think that the old one had through several years served a useful purpose, and would have continued to do so, if the land was not needed – I question that – which is food for thought.

But perhaps at some future date, it will maybe prove to have been a ghastly mistake.

And even though we continued to go out to the mud-flats – seeing as the place that we had frequented, with its acres of natural charm, had gone under the plough – it was never the same again.

But down there even now, away from the strains of modern living, I will be with you, among the crab strewn pools, or out at the water's edge.

Not far off from the last day at school, we were playing a game of rounders and one of the kids would not leave me alone, so I hit her with a rounders bat, and that was the last time – baring a few days – that I ever saw her, as far as I can remember. One has to stand up for oneself, doesn't one, which I did with great ease.

I'm afraid that I wasn't all that bright at anything really, and lessons came hard. Not once but several times two and two made seven. Hell, it would have been good for me if they had made anywhere near a five.

And I think that I would be right in saying that my geography was out of this world, and probably in the next. Where is France, I kept asking myself. 'Same place it's always been,' some bright spark piped up.

I suppose that I am English, but mastering the art of it was something else, and I still can't spell much without a visual aid of some sort, and history seemed a long way off to me – years back, in fact I am only just starting to get to grips with it. Ah well, it was all Greek to me anyway.

Late learners, isn't that what they call em? Well I would be a bit later than that – no, much later than that.

Still, it was a sad day when we had to leave, and would all sing 'All who are here shall meet no more.'

On reflection, I don't suppose that it was so bad, it won't come again, that's for sure.

Close the gate and keep me out, so as I won't be able to get back in again.

Wherever you are, my chums, I indeed wish you well.

The engine driver blew his whistle, and I jumped. Every time he got to Thorpe Culvert station he would blow the bloody whistle. I think that he knew that I was there. Of course we were there several Sundays throughout the summer, weather permitting.

Park up our bikes near a fence at the station, and wait for the steamers. We didn't have long to wait them days, as every few minutes one would come by, usually full of holiday makers on their way to Skegness, and others on the return journey, on the 'trip' trains, and my fingers were in my ears for most of the time.

What a wonderful sight it is watching an engine with its long train behind, chuffing down the track.

We were always telling Father that there was another train coming, and there wasn't much in the way of motor cars to spoil our enjoyment too much.

The bloke in the signal box probably thought 'here's that lot again,' and would probably go on to think 'Dad's had to bring em out to keep em still.'

Mind you, Dad didn't really care a bean, as the three of us would slowly wend our way through the same scenery, for several years.

'Well there won't be any more trains now, it's late, and the last one has gone,' Dad said. And we would want to stay a bit longer, as there might be a late arrival.

And one or other of us, on our way home, would glance back till the station was out of sight, because we might have missed one, and we often did.

I will cross the line on the odd occasion, but there are no more bikes there now, and our dear Father won't be taking us anymore. Only our spirits where we once trod.

The first time I went to the cinema was with Aunt Annie, and we cycled to Wainfleet. Before that time, and for a long time after, I would wonder why she only wore her stockings just above her knees. The very first time we ever went out on our bicycles, as I recall, the wind blew her skirt up, and for the very first time I realized that she wore her stockings just above her knees, held up with an elastic band. And I was hoping to God that the band didn't give way, for I was so sure that people could see under her skirt when the wind blew up in that direction. The embarrassment of it all when one is young!

But it seemed to be the dress code of the day, in my youth and before.

On the odd occasion, we would take ourselves off to visit an old lady, about a mile or so away, who wore a cloth flour-bag on her head – washed beforehand. She reminded me – remember that I was only about twelve at the time – of a witch. She would sit in a corner of the front room and not put on the light till it was fairly dark, and sitting in her rocking chair near the grate was just about all I could stand.

I should think that they were trying to save money, but I was glad to get out of there, even though the poor old thing did give me some toffees, and I suppose that she wasn't such a bad old thing after all, which was fairly easy to say when I got out of the place.

And on the way home, Aunt did say, 'Aren't you going to

eat one of your toffees, Seal?' – funny nickname, but then she always called me that.

'No, I don't think so,' I said, 'she looks a witch to me.'

'Sh . . . now you mustn't talk like that,' Auntie replied.

Didn't eat em though, they went straight into the fire when I got home.

The day Auntie ran out of 'wire' for making paper flowers, I found some in a drawer, and suggested we could use it. 'It' being fuse-wire, Auntie promptly replied that she didn't want to get an electric shock, so I put the card back in the drawer – still not forgotten.

I spent many happy hours there, having a go on the old organ, with the two pedals and several stops on either side. It had been given to her by a relative and it most certainly got a decent home, as we kept the old gal going.

Uncle Fred's teasing will not bother me anymore, nor will Auntie's stockings, they will be on a different 'high note'.

I got pneumonia as a nipper, and the local doctor paid a visit, just before he was about to leave for the services – that very day in fact – and managed to pull me through, and for that I am grateful.

Not unlike the Salvation Army who stopped outside our house on their way to the Friskney chapel, one time. I was in bed with some illness or other, and we could hear them coming down the road, so Mother ran outside to stop them before they got past. And I suppose that they thought I was on my last legs and, 'she's not here for long' – I can hear them now, playing for yours truly.

God knows what I would have thought if they had played

'Nearer my God to thee', which would not have exactly fitted me up for life.

But I have to say that I never forgot the day they arrived, and they do a wonderful job, and for that I thank them.

Can't remember if the day dawned bright and early, or not, but we will say it did, just for argument's sake. Anyway the bus picked me up, and I took my seat – can't remember who I sat next to – and off we went on a journey to the other side of the world – well it seemed like it at the time, not having travelled very far in those days.

I would be about fourteen at the time, and the trip was organized by the 'C of E' school. We were to stay at a youth hostel for the night and travel to various places during the day, which to me seemed rather exciting.

Everything went smoothly for several miles, and thinking about being sick never crossed my mind – it would do though, it would do.

Taking in the sights seemed to take my mind off things for several hours, but the movement of the bus, and it was getting hilly, and somehow I started not to notice the scenery anymore – which wasn't a good thing at all.

The hills were getting a lot bigger, and I was feeling a lot sicker – getting worse a bit at a time.

We were on our way to Lancashire of all places, to take in the sights of the docks at Liverpool, and then to a printing works at Manchester, with a bit of hill-walking thrown in for good measure.

I had always been a bad traveller, and looking at a large sign that said 'Snake Pass' didn't exactly help matters much, what with the mist looking as if it had just come out of a 'Hammer' film.

Halfway across the pass, or somewhere in that region, up from the seat – I'll swear that the aisle was a mile long – little ole me took herself off to the door and, with the mind all of a blur, flung the door open . . . and the windows were needing a good clean after that – one side of the bus was mistier than the other. Mind you, I felt a lot better for it, I can tell you.

You should have seen the side of the bus when we got off, the driver had to clean it himself.

'You mucky little sod,' he said. Never liked him after that, and wished him dead several times.

Think that it was the same day that we went round to the docks, and trust me to dangle my hands in the water, while hanging out of the cabin cruiser window.

Great big steel doors would close behind us as we entered a dry dock, and the water rose steadily to a certain level – an eerie experience.

After the Manchester printing works, which I can't say was all that exciting – although I did come away with a memento of the occasion, which I still have – it would be back to the youth hostel, where they would laugh at me for not wanting to take my clothes off to get into my winceyette pyjamas. I was a bit on the thin side, and had a starved look about me.

I wanted a bottom bunk – being scared of heights – but they wouldn't let me have one. One of them did finally relent, and let me take a bottom one. They were all laughing when I said that I was going to keep my vest on and I felt a right twit, I can tell you.

Sunday morning, going hill-climbing – they did, I didn't.

We arrived somewhere out in the countryside, and I took one look at the range of hills, and decided that I would stay at the bottom. One of the teachers had to stay with me and she didn't like it one little bit.

The others went off into the distance, gradually climbing up the steep grass-covered slope, while I had to stay at the bottom, twiddling my thumbs, a sorry sight indeed.

Then it was back to base camp, and the return journey home, and back over the pass, and I wasn't sick, but it wouldn't have taken much to have made me.

We stopped somewhere for fish and chips and, I had to tell them that I would have some – it was only because I dare not tell them that I didn't want any. I managed to eat some of it and promptly put the rest in my suitcase along with my weekend attire. Now on opening the case when I got home, doesn't leave a lot to the imagination.

One day I might go again under the Mersey tunnel.

Where they rest from their labours

Author's home village scene

Village draining ditch, where many a cycle accident was waiting to happen

Footpath where the sugar beet had seen the sharp edge of Father's knife

Friskney parish church tower, the base of the tower being Norman in origin

Hay making in the late forties

Local 18th century cottage

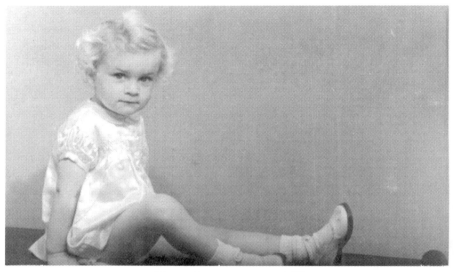

The author as a young child

Station in a nearby village, where many a steam train would blow

Horse and dray at 'Friskney School Feast' during the early 50's – a yearly event

The author's late Father, and her younger sibling (The Three Musketeers)

III

Fun and Games and Furry Friends

'I'm waiting for Santa Claus' I said to an aunt of mine one Christmas eve. 'Oh he's coming up the road, somewhere near the crossroads, he's in a green van,' she said. And for some strange reason, I believed her. Not that I was able to disagree, being only very young at the time – funny how the grown-ups would fob us off with stories like that. And it would be years after that I realized that it was Father who would tip-toe round the bed, probably aware that I had spotted him, in the early morning. Books and toys, and all manner of things some even now I have not had the heart to throw away, nor will I. There never seemed to be enough in the old pillowcase.

Albert would come to visit a relative close to where we lived, and we got to know him fairly well, and seeing that he was several years older than Bruce and me, he would have the upper hand.

He would be paying a visit to his dear Grandma, who lived next door to Uncle Sol, and the two of us would go across the field to have a word with him. Can't think why, we would usually arrive home the worse for wear, seeing as how he would tease us something rotten.

We would be only a short distance away, but watching his every move, as he would take a bicycle pump and put it in the 'toilet' water, first pushing in the handle, and then turn round and see us there watching – not that he didn't know that we were there all the time.

Somewhere on the turn, we would start to run away, with him chasing us and, pushing the pump handle in all the time and, he would eventually catch us, and cover us with the contents that he had sucked up from the toilet at Uncle Sol's.

I don't suppose that we were bothered much, as he chased us round Sol's house, 'firing' at us at every opportunity that he got and, we would go home stinking like a 'fummard' or polecat. I haven't seen him since the early fifties. Maybe I will somewhere on the turn.

There was a loud creaking noise in the corner of the living room, just under the piano – iron frame, and candlesticks, as it started to topple over backwards, and to the right, and lobbing itself against the wall. It was a bit too heavy for the floor which had given way, and there was a struggle trying to get it up again.

Someone came to repair the floorboards, and it held for a few more years before going out of tune. Then it was thought to need a lot of repair work which was going to cost a lot, but I carried on using it, and it was beginning to sound more like a harpsichord than a piano. Sounded more like a lot of mice running about in the back.

I learned to play the thing at about ten years old, and carried on till I was nearly fifteen, and not too long after that it would be taken apart, and spend the rest of its days in the shed till it was finally consumed by fire – I did keep the candlesticks.

Mrs Dunn, the local pianoforte teacher, managed to knock

some sense into me, and saw me well on the way to becoming the 'Liberace' of the keyboard. But as the youth in me subsided, and other things were taking over – boys – I lost interest and, didn't bother to get another one – piano that is – for several more years, by which time I had nearly lost interest and forgotten where everything was, and would have to start all over again – all the notes looked the same to me.

I thought it was like riding a bike, but with a lot of perseverance I found out, by asking around, where the 'G' was, and the rest, in time, came into place. And now, it does sound like a lot of mice running about.

Somewhere as near as dammit, some of my time would be spent in the school-yard corner, near the road – a few of us had a special spot.

It could have been something to do with the fact that I was maybe, just maybe, thought to be not all there, a bit on the silly side. Pure logic has often swung in my favour, hence me standing in the corner for hours at a time.

I remember lots of strange sounds would be coming from behind the bike shed and, I wouldn't have a clue as to what they were doing – the rotten lot never asked me to partake in their goings-on and it was left to some time after, to a short 'how's yer Father' down the sea bank. No good thinking about spiders down there, it was too bloody cold for that sometimes. Best thing was to just lie back and think of England. I should think that I was probably meant to enjoy it, if he had explained what was going on. I hadn't a bloody clue. Wasn't something supposed to fit somewhere, how silly of me not knowing. And now though it's the 'European Union' you lot need to think about, as you all lie there amid the sea-bank grasses and the purple heathers. Well, I have now learned how to connect the two pieces together, one way or another. And, can you tell me what all the excitement is about? I might be missing the point, so to speak.

There are plenty of good books on the top shelves – I needed a stool to stand on. And we were taught 'where we come from' at the school, but I hadn't a bloody clue what it was about.

And I might just as well have been standing in my corner of the school yard.

I'm just too old now, after a spell of devoted service, to remember how all these things are done – what was it I did.

We did keep, at one time or another, nearly every fur and feathered creature that could be called a pet – mostly small.

There was a duck that always seemed to know when we were going to arrive home, and he would arrive at the gate to meet us. Funny how he got the time right – probably with his 'mickey mouse' watch.

Rabbits all over the place, and one particular one, an angora, that sadly we parted with. The chap who we gave it to had only just left our house when he in turn gave it away to someone else who, as luck would have it, just happened to be passing our house at the time – can't say that I have thought much about him since.

Nearly every sort of chicken has passed through our lives, especially the 'Two Fudges'. I've no idea what their real names were but, they, like the rest of the brood, had the run of the place – not the house, the yard. Please don't get the wrong idea, and think that they were crapping all over the carpet.

Through the years that followed, they would all find their way to the after-life and I shall see them again.

40

Dad came into the house one day and said that one of them had fallen from its perch, dead, and it was my favourite, it always had a fluffy behind. Then I suppose that the rest of them did as well, when they hadn't got a bout of the runs. But on saying that, they were all well fed and housed.

I said I was going to drown my kids in the cistern outside our back door if I ever had any, and a school chum I remember telling that to, kept a respectable way off me for a long time.

Seeing as how I would only be about twelve at the time, I don't expect that it was likely to happen, but it would be about then that I turned my attention to furry companions instead. Happy days.

This particular day, Pauline Read, and I – she was staying with her Gran, Holly, for a few days – got on our bicycles to go to the village shop, just over a mile away, to get my Mother's weekly grocery list filled.

After filling two or three shopping bags – none of your plastic stuff in those days – we would head home back down field lane, and I should think that we would be about half-way down, when two bloody great big planes came over the top of us and scared us half to death. I didn't have a chance to bung up my ears and had to put up with it, with a few expletives thrown in for good measure.

Getting back down to the Eaudykes where I lived and where Pauline was staying not too far from our place, she would continue on with me to help with the shopping, seeing as she was carrying half of it on her handlebars.

She turned left, just in front of me, to go over to our old footbridge across the dyke at the front of our place, and didn't quite make it. Leaning too far to the left, she fell over the edge

41

of the bridge into the dyke, narrowly missing the water pipe. It would be a drop of about five feet, and along with her bicycle and the shopping, she caused quite a stir.

As soon as I saw what had happened, I raced up the path to get my Mother and Father, and the three of us went back down the path to see what, if anything, came crawling out.

We need not have worried, for as soon as we arrived, Pauline came out of the dyke, covered in mud, but reasonably okay, even if the shopping wasn't. I suppose that we would rescue some of it.

I can see her now, going over the edge, 'arse over tip' into the dyke.

Several years would elapse before we would see each other again.

The water pipe is no longer visible, having been covered over with a not so romantic tunnel. But then the footbridge was never much good from the point of view of safety. Pity really.

It was only a short distance from our place to where the Goodacres lived, and, when I was old enough, I would go most days for a jug of milk from their own cows, and usually arrive home with my thumb in the top of the milk – there didn't seem to be any other place to put it.

They would supply us and several of the locals with milk and butter, and would be a life-line in times of need, during and after the war years.

Father took Bruce and me to see the first 'milking machine' that Mr Goodacre had acquired. It would make the job of milking a lot better, and certainly be easier than sitting on a three-legged stool.

Mr Goodacre's cows knew exactly where to go on leaving

their home territory for a field some distance away, and do the same in reverse in the afternoon, in time for milking.

Seemed a daft idea to me, until it was explained. Several would be turning over to more modern machinery in my childhood.

Now though a lot of the charm has been taken out of it, as the 'English' cow seems to be made redundant and the bottled variety doesn't have the same appeal.

Mother would on occasion help the Goodacre's in getting a pig 'out of the way', which would ensure a reasonable amount of meat for several months – something else that is not done so often these days.

Neighbour would befriend neighbour, in a different age. Sadly, also not so apparent these days.

'Bramble canes' were much in use and, along with their own home-grown produce, in the form of vegetables, they would always have a regular food supply. And a few slices cut from the side of bacon would go down a treat with eggs from their own chickens.

The wind whips through the empty stalls, with long dead occupants in the spider's webs. And I don't think that I should be the least bit alarmed if I should come across the milking stool, in its original position.

One day Father came home looking not all that worse for wear, more, I would say, in a cheerful frame of mind.

Having just been to a funeral, as one of the bearers – it was something that he often did – I would have thought that he should have been a bit more sombre. Instead he was decidedly jolly, and not without good reason.

It would appear that when the coffin was almost at the bottom of the earth grave, the weather being a bit on the inclement side, the ground was particularly wet, so much so, that one of the bearers fell in on top of the coffin, and came scrambling out of the said place. Much to the delight of my dear Father, who would, I can imagine, have a struggle trying to retain his composure.

The chap in question was a bit on the tall side, and would usually be a bearer with Father, who would be a few inches shorter.

'Shoulder high' would be the norm those days – well mostly – and Father would have to keep 'hitching' himself to a higher position to gain control of whoever he was carrying at the time.

When Father passed away, he was so deserving of the same treatment, but had to make do with the services of a somewhat expandable afternoon dinner trolley.

Making one's own amusement came quite easily, as there wasn't anything in the way in the shape of electrical gadgets to distract us.

Several attempts were made by Father, trying his best with what skill he had, in making a 'kite'. A few left the earth, descending at a much greater speed, and any attempt at reviving them was useless. So it was back to the drawing board. We knew where we had gone wrong, but aerodynamics wasn't a strong point.

This might continue for a few hours, until Father, usually a cool man, would lose it altogether. Perhaps only till the next week. Seven days would give him time to cool off. While we, on the other hand, had turned our attention to more pressing matters.

The pig's bladder skimmed away, precariously, down the

cinder path, with us running after it.

This was our new pastime. A substitute, but certainly a lot cheaper than the real thing. And if it didn't get snagged with a sharp cinder, then it might last for weeks.

Sadly there are no more kites, and certainly pig's bladders are unavailable.

A breeze is beginning, just the weather . . .

My late brother, Roy, for whom I had the greatest affection, would chase me round the dining room table when I would aggravate him with the words of his not so favourite song. 'Be my life's companion, and you'll never grow old.'

Him being of portly appearance, I, a bit on the lean side, managed to move much quicker, much to everyone's disgust.

Time would see that we would change one life-style for another, and we would all go our separate ways.

And the table. I still have the table.

My younger brother Bruce and his friend stood in front of the house where they were about to have their picture taken, and someone asked Bruce if he would mind going into the house to change his trousers, as they had holes in both knees; whereupon his friend replied, 'Don't worry about that, I have got a hole in my trouser bottom.'

They would stay mates for years, until they would outgrow each other, and leave their go-carting days behind them.

The fruit on Audrey Chapman's gooseberry bushes was out of this world.

Nancy and I would munch our way through several at a time, along with Glenda, who would keep us all amused with a stream of bad verse.

The 'play-house' would see whoever got into it, all nicely seated, usually a scramble getting there first.

A well tended garden, which did not give its secrets up all that easily, with its twists and turns.

In my youth, and up to the present time, I have spent my rural pastimes there.

The golden drops haven't been around for several years, much like the old play-house under the poplar tree. It fell into disrepair after giving pleasure, and perhaps the odd squabble, during my youth and theirs.

1947 had seen my brother and I making 'caves' in the ditch behind our home.

The snow would last for several weeks, with impassable roads, and a non-existent electricity supply.

I don't suppose though that we had any idea as to how our parents were making out, in a trying time.

'Don't chuck too much coal on the fire, we shan't be getting any more for weeks,' Father was heard to say.

With a bit of foresight, one would be able to have a well-stocked larder, just in case, as there would be no question of going to the local town, and one would expect that the local store would be running low of supplies.

The snowman would stare at us with his cinder-made eyes, and it was a bad sign when he made no effort to melt. Not that we were really all that bothered. Any sign of melting snow would mean that we would have to go back to the infant school.

The bitter easterlies that had created the really adverse weather did subside eventually, only to be replaced by too much water, which wasn't half as exciting.

And with a thoroughly broken heart, I would watch as my inanimate friend would slowly melt away.

There have been one or two incidents of bad weather since but nothing on such a grand scale. And I would expect that we are long overdue for such an event.

B.S. was always better at 'marbles' than me. Being a lot larger, probably meant that she had a slight advantage over me.

But no, I think skill also played a part. The 'playing field' was very much pock-marked with holes of various sizes. And my 'glass allys' had the misfortune to disappear into one, if not all of them.

A sad time indeed, for at the end of the school term, I would be left scraping the bottom of the barrel. There might have been a marble in the corner of my pocket and, often there was. Just to get me out of feeling a complete loser.

You needed a keen eye, and a good sense of direction, if you intended to excel at the game. I was sadly lacking in both of these qualities.

Just a little way over to the left, or perhaps right, might have made an impression. Several 'pre-emptive' strikes, by B.S. saw to it, that it would be a futile gesture by me to carry on.

Still with true sportsmanship, I carried the flag for the Friskney team.

Dear Father passed away in 1975, and Mother in 1998. Brother Roy left us seven months before Mother, and Audrey would give her life to God, just over two years after. Uncle Sol, and Holly have long since gone to meet their maker. And Aunt Annie, and Uncle Fred left this earthly life, for a much greater calling.

And I am forever mindful of many others who have taken the same path.